PLENTY OF ROOM ON THE SHELF

PLENTY OF ROOM ON THE SHELF

A Guide to Self-Growth

STEPHANIE REMY

GROUPE

Stephanie Remy

Contents

INSPIRATIONAL QUOTES

To all the members of my Cheering Section, this one is totally for you.

So many of you profoundly believe in me.

I hear you, I see you, and for that, I Thank You!

To my late mother Cilianne, who always knew I was intended to be a beacon of hope and a light in this world. Thank you for always cheering!

Introduction

In a world brimming with boundless possibilities, where dreams have the power to shape destinies, every individual has a rightful place to thrive and excel. It is within this realm of infinite potential that the notion of success emerges as a beacon of hope, and aspirations. Often clouded by self-doubt and the shadows of others' achievements, we may momentarily forget that there is an abundance of room on the shelf, including the spot dedicated for us to thrive and flourish.

This preface aims to illuminate the significance of self-belief and resilience, to empower you with the conviction that your unique journey holds the promise of success. Success reserved for you and intended to fit your life only.

Within the wide array of differences in human existence, there exists a life that is similar to a star in the galaxy. A life that shines upon the universe with its distinct brilliance. Just as no two stars are identical, no two paths to success are the same. The symphony of life is composed of countless melodies, each contributing a harmonious note to the chorus of existence. It is crucial to remember that your story, your experiences, and your aspirations are what set you apart and make your journey a masterpiece of its own.

The seeds of greatness reside within every individual, awaiting the nurturing touch of self-assurance and resilience. Understandably, the path to success may consist of countless obstacles and challenges, but these trials and tribulations are not indicators of one being inadequate. On the contrary, they serve as stepping stones, honing in on the resilience and strength that will eventually lead you to the realization of your true potential. Embrace these challenges, for they are opportunities for growth and self-discovery, propelling you closer to your dreams.

In a world often compounded with comparisons, it is natural to question whether there is indeed room for your aspirations among the multitude of talents and achievements displayed by others. But consider this: the journey to success is not a comparison to zero game where one's triumphs come at the expense of another's. Each success story adds to the collective foundation of inspiration, igniting the flames of ambition in others. In this interconnected world, every success can serve as a stepping stone for someone else to rise and shine. Embrace the truth that your success will be a testament to the endless possibilities that life offers, and a vision of hope and inspiration for those seeking it.

As human beings, we have an innate capacity to forge connections with others, to build bridges of support and camaraderie. Surround yourself with those who uplift and inspire you, for their encouragement can fuel your determination and ignite the sparks of creativity within. Remember that success is rarely achieved in isolation; it is often a collaborative effort, where like-minded souls come together to achieve greatness. Surround yourself with a network of positive influences, where each member uplifts and supports the other, fostering an environment of growth and encouragement.

Beyond the realm of tangible achievements, success encompasses the journey of self-discovery and personal growth. Along this path, one learns to appreciate the beauty of resilience and the profound lessons hidden within setbacks. Drive and Determination get you here. Your journey may be unclear but it is the twists and turns that shape your character, building you up with the wisdom needed to conquer new frontiers. Trust in the power of your experiences and embrace the uncertainty, for it is in those moments that you will discover the strength that lies dormant within you.

A flower does not bloom overnight, and the night sky does not reveal its beauty in the absence of darkness. Similarly, success requires patience, perseverance, and unwavering dedication. Progress may appear gradual, but every step taken in pursuit of your dreams is a triumph in itself. Acknowledge your progress, no matter how small, for it is the foundation on which greatness is built.

Dear reader, in the wide array of experiences you will have in this world, do know that there is a place reserved just for you. A space to thrive, succeed, and make an impacting mark on the world around you. Embrace the uniqueness of your journey, celebrate the accomplishments of others as a testament on what is possible, and hold on to the belief that success is not the privilege of the elite, but the birthright of all who dare to dream, persevere and put in the hard-work. As we embark on this life path of exploration and self-realization, let us remember that within each of us lies the power to create a legacy that will positively impact the human existence but mostly allow such legacy to live on for generations to come. Embrace the boundless horizons that await you, and let the journey begin TODAY.

Okay, OK, that's all for the deep, serious stuff, let's get into the raw and bare bones this book is all about.

There is no need to envy someone else in the aisle, you have a spot on the shelf and the reservation has just your name on it.

STEPHANIE REMY

PLENTY OF ROOM ON THE SHELF

I

Make Note

And the very hairs on your head are numbered. So don't be afraid; you are more valuable to God than a whole flock of sparrows." Luke 12:7 NLT

Let's take some notes.

How easy it is to compare self to others. In doing this we often lose sight of the greatness of our present state and the truly positive aspects of our own lives. The thought of being worthy, yet unaccomplished can cripple progression and increase doubt. Comparison can fuel so many negative emotions but it can also negatively impact the state of mind. You can easily go from happy, to sad and angry by merely comparing self to others.

Feeling jealous of someone else's success can be counterproductive and emotionally draining. It's essential to maintain a positive mindset and focus on our own journey. Here are five other emotions to be conscious of an avoid when viewing the accomplishments of others.:

Envy: Envy is similar to jealousy but can be even more intense. Feeling envious of someone else's achievements can lead to negative thoughts and behaviors. Instead of dwelling on what others have accomplished, focus on your own strengths and work towards your own goals.

Resentment: Feeling resentful towards someone's success can create bitterness and hinder your ability to build meaningful relationships. Instead, practice celebrating their accomplishments and use them as inspiration for your own growth.

Inferiority: Comparing yourself unfavorably to others can lead to feelings of inadequacy. Remember that everyone has their own unique path, and your journey is just as valuable as anyone else's. Embrace your strengths and work on improving areas where you feel less confident.

Self-doubt: Witnessing someone else's success can trigger self-doubt, making you question your abilities and potential. Instead of doubting yourself, focus on your progress and how you can continue to improve and achieve your own goals.

Resignation: Feeling defeated because someone else has achieved something you desire can be demotivating. Use their accomplishments as a reminder that success is possible and that **you can also** achieve your dreams with determination and hard work.

Ultimately, it's crucial to maintain a healthy and positive mindset when observing another person's achievements. Embrace a growth-oriented perspective, celebrate their successes, and use them as motivation to strive for your own accomplishments. Everyone's journey is unique, and comparing yourself to others can distract you from fulfilling your potential and finding happiness in your own achievements.

I suggest you check yourself. In the moments when these feelings start to build and you haven't the slightest idea why, fall in line. In any and everything you do, your one and only competition is you. I do mean any and everything. If you are a business owner work to make your brand better to continue satisfying your consumer. They are what matter to you and what matters today is "how do we make the business a bit better than it was yesterday." Yes, bit by bit. No need to look at what another business owner is doing to fuel inferiority and thoughts of inadequacy. While it is great to be inspired, do not feel compelled to do the same or even challenged by them. Stay in your lane, you have your spot.

Same goes if you are a parent. No two children are alike, even if they are in the same household. Therefore, your parenting style and success need not reflect that of another. You will face different challenges and overcome them differently. The children will be receptive to different styles and response, that is to be expected. So again, no need to compare, no need to feel envy or even in competition with another parent. None of you are the same. Do your best with what you have, put in the honest effort and reap the good results. Simple.

In regard to career, so many want to move up and be promoted. Some find themselves stuck in a state of comparison and even resentment of peers and colleagues who receive acknowledgements and even praise for performance. Stay in your lane. Even when the comparison is made pointing out what you and/or said colleague can and cannot do well, stay in your line. Do not allow the success of another or even the recognition of their hard work be a source of discouragement for you. Continue to do what you are good at and do great at it, work diligently to always do better and grow in the process. Strive to perfect what you do and look to perform better every single day. See no competition besides your mirror reflection. Make note of your own wins, then double down and make them bigger and better.

In the back of this book are four pages Titled "**Self-Noted**" with subtitles on each page titled **Issue – Lesson – Resolve – Change.** Use that now to note the top 3 (three) issues you are able to identify about yourself.

From there write a lesson you once took from having that issue. For example: a time when you yourself were able to realize "wait something about that is not positive." Maybe it was a response you gave to a loved one in haste and realized it was an overreaction. Or maybe a time when a friend shared good news with you and you were not happy for them, and instead wished it was your news. Taking away a lesson from an issue is valuable in growth.

This is your first task.

Write down an issue, the lesson you took away from it, what you did to resolve it or what you can do to correct it so it doesn't happen again. Come back to the page when you have finished this book and identify using (Yes/No) on the change page, to note if you have or have not changed from the issue. Having understood the concepts shared in the book how will you handle things moving forward? So, with a fresh state of mind the question will then be, "have you changed the way you think now?"

You will also find areas to make note of things you are proud of, because there are so many. Do not be afraid to note the little wins, a win is a win. There is also an area to recognize some of the key resources in your life, your cheering squad. Making note of these people will offer you a reference on who to call on when you need a gentle reminder on cloudy days of the mind. First read about the role they play, so you can best be able to identify them in your life.

You will need to make note of some goals and objectives. After reading this book, or even as you are reading, make notes of ideas that spark. Be inspired so much that you fill it with goals and objectives that you intend to accomplish. Now knowing how to put in the work, why to keep going, and the preparation for your spot on the shelf, you will realize goals are important. Big or small, make note of them because they matter.

"If you listen to these commands of the Lord your God that I am giving you today, and if you carefully obey them, the Lord will make you the head and not the tail, and you will always be on top and never at the bottom." Deuteronomy 28:13 NLT

This little "Life" of yours, Through it you will shine. No darkness or clouds can block what's YOURS!

STEPHANIE REMY

PLENTY OF ROOM ON THE SHELF

II

Life-Print

"I Knew you before I formed you in your mother's womb. Before you were born, I set you apart." Jeremiah 1:5

Your life was designed for greatness long before anyone knew you would exist. Today it is yours to live out in the greatness of your own being.

What defines you? What makes sense in your life today? It is easy to have no right answers to such questions. It is even easier to just not know at all. You have a Life-Print, it is a mark you've made on the world whether you believe it or not, it exists.

What's life got to do with it?

Think long and hard on that answer. Everything.

"Life" is an introduction on what you are about to embark on in this book. I will share with you, explanations on why you should never feel like the underdog, and reasons why you should never feel like you can't follow your dreams. I am certain there may have

been wonderful ideas in your mind, that you may have thought up, dreams and goals you imagined, all of which may have been quickly shut down. Whether by fear or self-doubt, in one way or another it was here today and gone tomorrow.

There may have even more likely been countless people who told you that some wondrous thing you shared with them was impossible. Many may have discouraged you with their words or banter so much that you decided to retreat, remove the thought and return to your reality. Casting their fears and self-doubt onto you, and producing that same result from you. Far too many people exist who are so afraid to start anything, so much that they bring others down and stop them from starting also. People will have their own perspectives and expectations of themselves. These same people may also believe what is good for them, is also what is good for you. Not the case. Don't buy into that rhetoric.

On a different note, maybe you are someone who has always been told how great you would be at something, but you just never saw it in yourself. That is ok. That is why I decided to print this book as a resourceful guide and reminder.

A little something to help boost your confidence, on why there should be nothing that stops or keeps you from your dreams.

Keep moving forward and don't look back. Ever!

If leaving a legacy is something you aspire to, or even if feeling accomplished is a goal you have for self, there is a likelihood it is already part of your Life-Print. It is said that everything happens for a reason and it is our life experiences that shape us, this is quite truthful.

There are so many reasons why the dream you have can change the world, and even if not globally, but it can most certainly shape and change your world. Something in you was gifted to be shared with the world. Or maybe even to inspire those in your world whom you may or may not even know. It is so hard to get unstuck, once you get stuck. Hard to regain focus once you've lost it, and even harder to get back on track when you've lost your way.

The goal here is to help you with some insight on what to do and what not to do. Also, both things to watch for and things to acknowledge, will all be identified to assist you. Far too often we overlook what is right in front of us, and their intrinsic values are outwardly missed by our naked eye.

You will learn how to set your sights on everything around you that can help sustain, maintain and elevate you. You will also be able to identify the types of people to avoid. Most importantly this book will remind you that there exists plenty of room on the shelf, including a spot designated just for you. You have a Master blueprint that was put together long before your birth. It is designed as your Life-Print and everything that is destined for you, will always be reserved just for you, because it is already yours. You just haven't uncovered it yet. This includes a seat at the table and that spot front and center on the shelf.

Take from your life experiences everything that is offered to you. Make of your own life everything that makes you feel fulfilled and happy. If it means something to you, there is no doubt you will work hard at uncovering it and bringing it to life in front of the world. Of the billions of people in this world, each one has a special gift to share. A specific task they are uniquely required to complete. You are nothing like the rest just as no two people are alike. Even identical twins have differences in personality, appearance and even life path.

You will walk alone, remember this. There will be moments when no one wants to walk with you. That is ok. You are not intended to walk the same roads. You must always keep going. Keeping in mind, the vision was given to you, the goal is yours, and it is up to you to bring it to life for the world to see. So even if your vision was sparked by something already out there, use what is in that vision to make all the changes you see necessary. Think about this, someone invented regular flat shoes. Another person invented athletic sneakers. Another person invented laces. Another person invented heels. Yet still, different kinds of laces exist. Just as different styles of shoes, heels and sneakers are making their rounds all over the world. This little fact here, means your contribution counts.

It is through your life-print you will make your mark on this world. Everything you need to succeed you are already fully equipped with. Activate your faith, believe in yourself but also let the Most-High lead the way. After all, He knew you and the plans He had for you long before you landed in your mother's womb. So, trust and keep hope and faith.

"For I know the plans I have for you. They are plans for good and not for disaster, to give you a future and a hope." Jeremiah 29:11 NLT

It is all in what you make of it.
Oh what a "beautiful" life!

No two roads are alike.
So, stop expecting your journey to look like anyone else's. Your challenges and obstacles may appear similar but they are not the same.

STEPHANIE REMY

PLENTY OF ROOM ON THE SHELF

III

The Journey

"When you go through deep waters, I will be with you. When you go through rivers of difficulty, you will not drown. When you walk through the fire of oppression, you will not be burned up; the flames will not consume you." Isaiah 43:2 NLT

What do we already know about this thing called life? Not much, I'd say. At least not enough to get through it on our own. We typically answer these questions by looking into what we are, who we are and how we handle things and each other. How far you've come and how far you look to go are also considerations made when evaluating the journey of our lives.

At this point we are all aware that life doesn't offer a user manual, or at least most of us have come to this realization. Life is that one thing that we must sojourn in order to learn the ins and outs on how best to navigate it. The whole "seeing is believing" or better yet walking miles and miles in your own shoes. Since there are no blueprints that demonstrate our finished product or even a how-to on producing it, we come to realize that everything just happens real time, over time.

Unlike road maps, you don't get a GPS navigation system to direct you and keep you on track. Nothing ahead of your path that helps indicate which turn will have the most traffic or hazards to avoid. Not even an alert that offers an alternate route which will get you there faster. Instead, you discover these things through your own experiences. The destination of your map is designed just for you, by you, and you realize this only as you go along. Just like this one, your life is your book along with the pen of experience in your hand. You walk the walk and write the pages as you go.

Do make note; never allow anyone to write on your pages, edit your story, make it their own, or remove pages, as that all takes away from the authenticity. Your authentic self. No two books are alike even if similarities exist, there are clear differences as well. You will find along the way, many people who want to rewrite your story, and make it look like their own. They may want you to mimic their life story and, walk in their shoes, even if they don't fit. Don't allow for that to happen because the road you walk, is uncharted until you've walked it. This meaning, your book pages are blank until you've taken the steps, which are seen as pen strokes transcribing every move on your journey. Trust that your Life-Print has something complete and custom designed just for you. This will help ensure clarity for you when others try and convince you that your journey is supposed to look like theirs. Trust me, it's NOT!

What we do have is our own blueprint called "Life-Print." This is the predestined way your life will go, sort of like a timeline. Your life-print was here prior to your conception and has all the steps on your journey mapped out. Including obstacles, triumphs, pains and joys. The roads you take that may turn out to be dead ends, are on there. People you meet who shape different things about your life are in your life-print. Those who stay the course and those who fall by the wayside are also characters within your story.

The thing about this life-print is that we just never get a chance to preview it, because we instead get the first-hand option to live it out.

As people we overcome and face many challenges, socially, academically, professionally and in our private lives. Far too many to be counted. This means that life is already filled with ups and downs. Even as a sub-group or culture we all face challenges every single day. The art of mastering them is in you.

We are all equipped to win and with that there are no losers. You'll meet people on your way placed as pieces to cheer you on. That's your cheering section. Other people will be placed as obstacles on your path. Those are your oppositions. And the one group we normally fail to notice are the ones placed beside you.

These are not your competitors but your fellows. You are all in it to win. You are running in the same race of life. The wonderful thing about the race of life is that there is not one winner. We can all win. The objective is merely a successful and happy ending.

Overcoming the obstacles and making it across the finish line are primary objectives. There are no timers, no point markers just a leveled playing field called 24 hours. We all start off with it every hour and every minute of the day.

Taking a look into what you are is the first step to understanding and cultivating who you are intended to be. The question at this point is likely "but how?"

Let's take a deeper look together and find exactly what it is we require to take the first step. This is the hardest step but it leads to the greatest results.

As a starting point we need to silence our minds at times, to hear the message from within. This should be the number one item on our mental checklist of things to do. It's not easy to silence the mind, as we have so much going on inside of it. So many thoughts, dreams, daily tasks, memories, joys and even disappointments.

Each one haunting in its very own way.

We get up every day with a mind that is always on GO. It starts off whether it be by the sound of an alarm or the hand of the almighty with a gentle nudge. Fact is once we wake, our minds are set and constantly absorbing new objectives. This particular reason is why it is rather difficult to silence the mind because everything going on inside of it, is loud noise. Sit quietly and listen for the voice within, listen for that conversation daily. It will help you with your journey.

It is an internal guide that will provide direction for your steps and direct or redirect them. We are all equipped with it, but we must silence the noise to hear it.

Otherwise, the road of life will be harder to navigate, and intuitive messages intended to push you ahead or divert you to a detour will often be missed. Identify the voice and it will help you through some challenges. It may even amplify the sounds of your cheering section.

Life was not intended to be easy and your journey although long and challenging has a story wrapped up in it. A story that will inspire others.

"Don't let your hearts be troubled. Trust in God, and also trust in me."
John 14:1 NLT

Somewhere out there, is someone looking at you with sincere admiration. They truly believe in you, and are cheering for you, so go on and inspire them!

STEPHANIE REMY

PLENTY OF ROOM ON THE SHELF

IV

⧬

Cheering Section

"There are "friends" who destroy each other, but a real friend sticks closer than a brother." Proverbs 18:24 NLT

Front row, floor seats or anywhere in the crowd you just can't miss them. They see the potential and they believe in you, sometimes more than you believe in yourself. These are the valuable people placed in your life with a purpose.

Welcome to your cheering section.

This group is comprised of all kinds of people. Members of this section can be a friend, a teacher, a co-worker, parent, family, neighbor or someone you just met. They all have one thing in common, they see and they believe in you. They trust in your greatness and are proud to watch it unfold.

Your cheering section members believe in you when you may not quite see your potential yet. They see the fire and they are drawn to the flame. They are tuned in and fully engaged. This group comes to the rescue during many turns and valleys in the road of life. You can look to them for affirmation on days when the objective is no longer clear. Strength and reassurance when things no longer make sense. Or even peace of mind when your mind refuses to silence. When in doubt, seek them out.

They push you through humps and hurdles because they know you can win. This especially when you no longer believe you will. Think of that friend that truly rejoices during your victories. Picture the smile they have and the words of power they use to build you up. They often say things like "I am so proud of you," or "I told you, you could do it." Now identify how genuine the delivery is and how reassuring it makes you feel. That family member whom, no matter how negative and doubtful others may speak about you, they stand in. No matter how much others stay away in avoidance of you, they remain ever present and constantly letting you know that you are able stating, "I know you can do it."

Everyone needs positive affirmations and reinforcement in life because this life thing can be discouraging and overwhelming all at once. It is good to have people around who help get you through the rough patches and out of the pitfalls. Every winning team has them. Popular name is fans, but in this book, they're known as the "Cheering Section."

Your cheering section has already helped you thus far in life in so many ways, they have already demonstrated their value and position. Members may have cried with you, shared their own hurt shamelessly with you, made themselves vulnerable in an effort to uplift you.

We need this group and their importance is clear in our lives even when we fail to immediately realize the strength in ourselves. It is far too easy to be discouraged and feel like giving up. The slightest mishaps in life when compounded can make us feel defeated. Sometimes it can feel like you just can't get a break. This leads to feelings of disappointment and discouragement. Look at your cheering-squad as the team of people that stand right outside of your corner of the ring in a boxing match. They tell you to get up, duck, keep going, great job. All because they believe in you. Imagine these are the voices heard when a boxer lies on the ring floor. "Get up, come on, you got this, just get up." Then they get up and continue the fight and even win. Everyone is equally proud in the end. You are happy with your victory, and the cheering-squad is so very proud of you. They knew you had it in you to win.

Look at life today and think for a second of five people who have positively influenced you or pushed you in a direction that was beneficial to you and not them. Use the back of this book to identify them. That selfish kind of love and care only comes from the cheering section. People who want to see you win even though it's not their race and they have no stake in the game. They are truly an inspiration and bearers of hope, see them as that. You are fortunate to have a strong support system. Each person was hand picked to bring something different to the table. Many will get you through to a certain point and others pick up from there to keep pushing you forward. Your cheering-section is like a rib! God knew you needed them so He provided.

Understand that not all members will be as loud as the others. Some you will already know you can call on even if they are not prominent and loud about things. You know these people as the ones that come to mind when you are in a bind, or when you feel like you are out of options. They will do whatever it takes to get you back on track, because they want to see you win. They will do anything to uplift and reinforce everything great about you that may have been displaced or attacked.

Valuable are these people and never lose sight of this fact. Hold them in a high regard, because they sincerely believe in you.

It is because life is not designed to be easy, that these people are placed in your life. They soften the blows of life and they often make things better. A warm hug, a shoulder to cry on and a boost in the right direction. You need every member of your cheering section and they each play an important role. It is one thing to travel the road of life alone, but with a support system, challenges are easier to overcome and self-doubt has a way of disappearing as well. You may be the member of someone else's cheering section. Think of how that makes you feel to inspire and push them, even when they don't see it in themselves and seem hopeless. You find a way to encourage them to go on and not give up. They need you. They rely on you and without you they may have missed many mile markers in life. So, see yourself not just as a receiver, but also as a giver of hope and light.

Move fearlessly knowing that there are eyes on you that are inspired by you. Navigate these waters and look to them for that good ole "wink and the gun" that brings a smile of confidence to your face. All of the ingredients you need to succeed are at your disposal. Your cheering squad is the Sugar, Honey, Ice, Tea.

A strong support system makes it easier to navigate in life. Not that challenges won't exist, just that the load will be less heavy.

The size of your cheering squad may vary. It may be one. It may be some. But the power they have to push you is mighty!

"The heartfelt counsel of a friend is as sweet as perfume and incense."
Proverbs 27:9 NLT

Eyes are watching.
Keep your eyes on the goal.

Not everyone will believe in your vision or your dream. Your only role is to ignore them and just make it happen. Seeing is the surest way to believing.

STEPHANIE REMY

PLENTY OF ROOM ON THE SHELF

V

Oppositions

"You prepare a feast for me in the presence of my enemies. You honor me by anointing my head with oil. My cup overflows with blessings." Psalms 23:5 NLT

As with any race this group serves as the obstacle course. They don't want to see you win. This group is placed in your life to teach you lessons through challenges. Challenges which you will overcome. Always take the lesson into account. Understand what you have already learned from a hurdle or challenge. A lesson which was presented by an opposer. Keep that drive and conscious knowledge front and center - that you have already won.

This is how you overcome.

This group set as an obstacle and can come into your life disguised as a friend or even a family member. They can be a teacher at school, a leader in your workplace or even someone you come across every day. You may be able to identify them in memories of your life accounts where they were present but absent. How can someone be present but absent you might ask? Well they can.

Someone who is there in your moment of sorrow but not as a comforter, instead as a spectator. Someone who isn't cheering but rather shushing the crowd. Someone who tells you everything that you're doing wrong and never reinforcing what you've done well or correctly.

That person who constantly looks to contradict your vision and your dreams in an attempt to fill you with self-doubt. You may not need to think hard, and have possibly already identified a few.

They are your oppositions.

Placed in your life to steer you away from your goals. Constantly discouraging you against what you have decided to follow, from within your heart. That is what they do.

They come disguised as friends to gain your trust. Another way to convince or persuade you. They will cheer quietly for your win only because they don't want to be outed in the crowd. All the while they are preying on your downfall. Their praises and kind words are never genuine and rather forced.

They are in your life to trip you up, veer you off course and in many instances hurt you to your failing point.

Be aware of this because you will see right through them, but doubt may make you believe that what you are seeing is not true. Know that when they trip you and you fall, you must never stay down. Get right back up. They may offer you a hand, if what they have done was noticed by others and act as if it was accidental. They will try again. This is what they are in your life for.

Remember life wasn't meant to be easy and your opposition will remind you of this at many points, in so many ways and on so many days.

You will come across people in life who have convinced themselves that they cannot win. DO NOT allow them to place those convictions on you. They may have decided not to carry on, to sit on the side of the road, or to just turn back believing they just won't make it if they continue.

DO NOT allow them to make you believe that this is also your fate. You are not on the same life journey because the steps you take as you write your life book are different.

The pebble you step on during your race may not be the same one they step on. The gust of wind that is brushing against your face, is not the same brushing against theirs. Know in your mind that no two journeys are intended to be the same, so don't let someone convince you to emulate their own.

Be aware what role these people are playing.

Are they sitting in your cheering section but have set obstacles in the form of discouragement on your path? An opposer may be hard to identify when they sit among those in your cheering section BUT they are often soon exposed.

The disingenuous sound of their cheer always sounds off. They cheer and discourage in the same breath. Be aware and alert to those warning signs. Anyone who attempts to divert your path without a positive reroute is likely an opposition.

We are human and we thrive off encouragement, but discouragement can also be a powerful dream killer. Your potential is known by you and may be evident to others. Not all want to see it manifest into greatness.

Remember there are just a few members in your cheering section.

It's not usually a magnitude but they are just as powerful. They have a strong force. So, expect that anyone outside of this group may be an opposition. Life is full of hurdles and we can now identify those as oppositions.

They may not be people; they may be situations and bad decisions. You just need to be able to identify the hurdle using discernment. Overcome it and note the lesson for future reference. But no matter what, just keep on moving.

"Instead, if your enemies are hungry, feed them. If they are thirsty, give them something to drink. In doing this, you will heap burning coals of shame on their head." Romans 12:20 NLT

They will ignore you.
They will see you.
They will doubt you.
They will laugh at you.
They will watch you grow.
They will admire you.
They will be inspired by you.
They will ask to join you.

By your side is where a lot of inspiration resides. Just as you too are an inspiration on someone else's side, in someone else's eyes.

STEPHANIE REMY

PLENTY OF ROOM ON THE SHELF

VI

Fellows

"How wonderful and pleasant it is when brothers live together in harmony!" Psalms 133:1 NLT

How do we understand a "Fellow" role? This is pretty simple, and comes with an accompanied state of mind. Your fellow is someone on the same journey as yourself. In too many instances these individuals are viewed as a threat.

Far too often though, they have run the same course as you have and overcame some of the same challenges.

Being envious or jealous of these individuals is never the right solution. Look at it like this, a fellow is someone you can learn from, or someone who can learn from you. You may be able to help each other avoid some mistakes you have already made, mistakes that may have kept you from succeeding in one way or another.

They can offer you the same insight and keep you from having to overcome unnecessary hurdles by leading through example as well.

Where people tend to lose and get tripped up, is when they view the fellows as a problem, thus internalizing them as a form of discouragement in many cases.

Let me explain.

When you are busy focused on how much further ahead someone has gotten than yourself, you lose focus on your objective. When you're busy counting their success, not even knowing what it took to get them there, you are doing a disservice to yourself. The truth remains that every journey is different and what is designed for you, will always end up in your hands.

"Focusing on what is going on beside you or behind you is never the way to the finish line."

Yes, your fellows run the same race as you do, but if you program your mind to look at things from a positive lens you won't miss the common objective.

Everyone just wants to finish the race and cross the finish line. That is the grand picture and primary objective in most aspects.

Yes, some may finish sooner than others. Others may even move at a faster pace, and leave you behind, but that should never allow you to deviate from the objective of – crossing the finish line.

When you start to view fellows as inspiration and examples, instead of competition your state of mind is different and the journey is often less hectic. I am telling you, and reminding you AGAIN, there is plenty of room on the shelf. When you make it across that finish line you too will have been identified as one of the many who "did" it.

There goes your recognition.

Allow yourself to be fueled off determination and a will to succeed. That will be what gets you where you're going. Success is in the process and the results it breeds. Not in the who was next to you and how you may have tripped them up. That is not the way.

Here is an example of a fellow, in the store aisle TIDE and ALL. Two different brands of laundry detergent found in the same store aisle, usually on the same shelves.

Let us a dive a little deeper. TIDE is owned by a company named Proctor and Gamble, and ALL owned by the Henkel Corporation.

Some days there aren't many TIDE detergents left on the shelf, just as there are days when the ALL brand is out as well. These two companies have been thriving for over 25 years, from my first-hand knowledge.

I can recall commercials for ALL on tv as a kid growing up, just as I can remember TIDE commercials as a teen.

They have both crossed the finish line with no regard for the other, besides possibly learning from each-others mistakes over time. Both brands have their own loyal group.

Whatever the reason may be. Could be the scent, the ingredients, the number of loads per gallon. It could even just be the familiarity of having used it for so long and keeping to what they know.

Your loyal group will be there and they will always choose you over the other.

Just as the others will have their own group that chooses them over you. Continue to provide for your group because they will always expect you to deliver for them.

My point is this, look how those two brands have made it. So can you. They sit right beside each other and they understand that they may face the same scrutiny on ingredients, on product safety, packaging, but they learn and grow.

Here is another example of a fellow, General Mills and Post. Some of you may love Honey Bunches of Oats, while others may love Honey Nut Cheerios. Two totally popular cereals, from two totally different brands. I can guarantee any store cereal aisle you walk down these two are there. They each have a loyal consumer that enjoys the quality, flavor or the value-added benefit they offer to them. For many years they have had a seat on the shelves, as have many other cereal brands and flavors.

Beyond just cereal, countless brands of the same nature and product delivery all exist, and have been that way for many years. I always challenge a new client who may feel discouraged that their product or service already exists, to take a walk down a store aisle. I require that they do this in many different stores like Target, Walmart, Trader Joes, Whole Foods, Macys and even Nordstrom to make notes. I ask that they note the different brands of items on the shelves, on the racks, on counters offering a similar product. From the sweaters that look similar but are from a different brand. Maybe the difference is that one is cotton and the other is polyester. Some people prefer cotton over polyester and vice versa. Therefore, BOTH brands are serving their consumer.

I ask that they pay attention even to the point of the checkout lane. Look at all the different brands of gum. Think of how long you've recognized each one, some many, many years now. They still have their spot on the shelf. Although a fellow brand sits right beside them, catering to their very own consumer. You have sugarfree, vegan, mint, peppermint and so many flavors that different brands offer. You always see them because they are always supplying their consumer. That is their objective.

So just as these brands continue to be, you do the same. Do not view your fellows as your competition, instead understand that you have something particular to offer your group and that is what "they" need. Support your fellows, just as you would expect them to support you. We are all in it to win, and no one can take what is reserved and set aside for you. Even if they were to steal it, one way or another it will end up right back in your hand! View your fellows as your peers. Both learning and growing and producing for their clients/consumers.

You need to understand this valuable piece to get ahead, and through the life course. There will be challenges. Keep your focus on getting through them and learn as you go. Your Fellow does not need to always be seen as a reason to give up, or even to get discouraged and/or upset by their growth.

Instead look at it this way, your tribe of loyals already exist and whatever you have to offer they are waiting for it. They are waiting for you!

"When we arrived, the brothers and sisters in Jerusalem welcomed us warmly." Acts 21:17 NLT

Let me make this very clear, set goals and objectives. Accomplish them, be inspired and set some more. Put no cap on how big you dream.

STEPHANIE REMY

PLENTY OF ROOM ON THE SHELF

VII

~❧~

Objectives

"Commit your actions to the Lord, and your plans will succeed."
Proverbs 16:3 NLT

You have to create objectives. Running blind is something we do, but having a plan is positive and in many ways, a better strategy. If you have a dream, map out how you plan on making it real. If you want to own a beauty shop, auto body shop, be a doctor or a lawyer, getting a degree or even just moving up in your current job to be comfortable. If it is what your heart and soul desires, it is your objective.

Okay, the truth is we can't always plan in life, but we can offer ourselves an idea. What we'd like to see, where we'd like to go. How we plan on attempting to get there are the things we can set in place. Things will not always go as planned. I repeat, things DO NOT always go as planned.

What we want will not always come to be, but we can give ourselves a starting point, and something to look forward to on our journey.

Be prepared for disappointments, because they come.

But don't let that discourage you from wanting to set and reach goals. Dream as big as you want, and know that if the stars don't align on what you wanted it may be because your destined life-print contained something better.

Often times we may miss that small fact. So many times, we set our heart on something and when we don't get it, we get discouraged. In those same instances we may have received something smaller but far more valuable and because of the size we don't see the true magnitude of its purpose.

Here's an example to help you understand.

You're in a position at your job and you constantly pray for a promotion to management. You see an opening and set your heart knowing that you deserve it and are more than qualified for the role.

You don't get it, instead a few months down the line you're offered a different position, one you've heard many others complain about and you feel as though this is unfair to you.

It isn't the management position but it offers decent pay and flexibility to your schedule as long as the work is complete. Now others in this role may not have been mentally equipped to excel in this role but you fit right in. You have a passion and never had time to explore it, but now you do.

You find the work challenging but you are efficient and get it done anyway. You complete it every time, and create space for that flexibility. You're still saying to yourself "I deserved that management job, can't believe I didn't get it." You're missing the magnitude of this smaller yet abundant opportunity.

You have the ability to pursue other dreams because you have the time. The manager has loads of files and paperwork, or barely gets free time besides scheduled vacation.

Here you are with the opportunity to capitalize on your passion and that alone may propel you into something bigger than that management job you set your heart on. You can end up managing your own company once you put more time into your passion. See how one can miss that small but immense blessing after being denied something else? Don't let that be you.

There are two groups of people in life.

One is no better than the other because we need both to get the job done. There are leaders who envision and create the job following through on their dream. And there are followers who get the job done, helping sustain that dream. What a lot of people fail to realize is that, both parties are equally valuable. You need the job to be created and not all the time can a single person get it done.

Leaders are the group of people who have the dream or the vision and jump through as many hoops of fire as needed to bring it to life. They have a drive and they capitalize on it.

They want to win and are willing to push, bleed and drag themselves no matter what and overcoming all oppositions, to get there is what they do.

Like I said before, there are no single winners. We can all win, but you've got to face the fear of the pain and the unknown. You have to push through the blood and the pain dragging yourself at times, because you believe in the dream. It seemed so real in your mind you want to do whatever it takes to bring it to life.

The followers keep the wheels rolling. They are provided with a set of rules, directions to follow on what to do, this is called a "job duty description." It breaks down what was in the mind of the visionary. It explains how to bring the dream to a reality and how to keep it alive. The follower knows the rules, and is willing to put their effort into keeping the wheels rolling.

They are not without dreams they may have just been too afraid to act on them.

That being said, they may have had a similar vision and are willing to help bring yours into fruition because they also see the potential. Remember we are two groups for a reason, one to envision and create, the other to execute and sustain. Fear of the unknown, and afraid to take the first step are reasons for the existence of followers.

But in that same reasoning, they are often believers and what I like to call helpers of the dream, so treat them as equals. I can tell you to decide which one you are, a Leader or follower but you are already subconsciously aware. In both instances you are still an asset.

My explanation is simple. A leader used their last chance on their dream. A follower played it safe, but believes in the leader's dream. One may be happiest as a corporation with an abundance of added responsibilities and as the leader they happily generate the paychecks. While many people are happy with the paycheck, minus all the added responsibilities of hierarchy.

Don't let anyone take your happiness from you. Always know at the end of the day it is the most important. So whatever it is, if it makes you happy and doesn't bring harm to others, DO IT!

You serve a purpose and either pay or get paid. Seats at the table are set and everyone eats. Keep your focus on your objectives and stick to what you want. Focus your mind on what you want to do. Use the energy of your cheering section to move forward and use it to push through.

Especially on days when you don't see the way to navigate and want to give up. DON'T!

On these days use the energy and belief in you from the cheering section to get you through the muddy patches that slow you down. They believe in you and some may even look up to you, do not disappoint them and you won't disappoint yourself either. Keep your eye on the prize of the objectives you've set.

"May He grant your hearts desires and make all your plans succeed."
Psalms 20:4 NLT

Identify why you're doing it all for, and identify it early.
Knowing your why, is the fuel that keeps your fire burning.

STEPHANIE REMY

PLENTY OF ROOM ON THE SHELF

VIII

Aisle 4

"I press on to reach the end of the race and receive the heavenly prize for which God, through Christ Jesus, is calling us." Philippians 3:14 NLT

My question here is what 4? What is your reason for wanting to be in this race?

How did you determine the objective and how did you find the supporting reasoning to pursue it?

You have decided you want your spot on the shelf and you are determined to get it. Here's a heads up, the path will not be easy, because things worth having don't normally come easy. Also, you will face all kinds of challenges and obstacles that will throw you off course. That's all in the grand scheme of things.

I need you to determine WHY you need to be on the shelf (key word here "need") and allow that to fuel you and push you through those challenging areas.

Aisle 4 is where you ask all the questions to yourself. Questions that once you answer will serve as a constant reminder as to why you go hard every day. For parents, they usually say their children are their why. Some people would like to make their parents proud, and that is their why. Others may want to offer themselves the feeling of accomplishing something because so many things may have gone wrong, and that is their why.

We all need a why, because those days will come when giving up seems like the only option and you will ask yourself "why am I even doing this?" Or "Why should I go on, if it isn't working?"

Having answered this question ahead of time, the answers will surely come.

And that will push you through.

It is important to identify your why and even share it with your cheerleaders, they will be happy to remind you, in case you forget. Here is another important WHY you need to answer. Why do it, when it's already out there? This why will also come and it will be accompanied by thoughts to discourage you in an attempt to make you believe your reasons are unsubstantial. Answer this why ahead of time also.

Maybe your why is because you have something special to offer. Identify how you can disrupt the norm and earn your spot on the shelf. Yes, everything may have already been done on this planet, but it hasn't been done your way and by the design in your mind.

Stand firm on your why, because the dream was yours and yours alone.

It is your job to bring it to life to show the world. Enhancements happen all the time. Things are constantly changing. You may be the one to offer a breakthrough on something extraordinary. Don't let a why keep you from that, instead go forward with the "why not?"

Why not try? If you fail, why not try again? Why not give it a fair shot as many times are needed?

It has always been intriguing and funny to me, how an infant is always far more optimistic and willing to challenge things in an effort to make it make sense. You know, the infamous why's, that came with every answer, their way of trying to make everything make sense.

Because to them can't was never an inherent understanding.

I have seen and had numerous conversations that have gone like this with infants. You can't go outside. "Why?" Because you need a jacket. "Why?" Because it's raining. "Why?" Because liquid precipitation was stored in the clouds. Why?' Then you struggle to make it make sense because now you're getting stuck. The reality is, they can go outside.

They may get wet and the rain will fall but your reasoning is not enough to make it make sense. Now picture this. A brave young infant opens the door and goes outside. They have now proven you wrong.

Have proven you wrong in a sense of the original can't – the saying "you can't go outside." They did, and while they got wet in the rain that wasn't reason enough to keep them from going outside.

I say all this to say, although you may be told how you can't and why you can't, never let that be the end all be all. There are so many ways to get to where you want to go. You can't allow anyone to keep you from it. Gather all the answers to your whys and keep them with you. They will always get you where you're going and they will always keep you going.

Today, do this important thing for yourself.

In the back of this book take a moment to write down all the answers to your why.

Recite them every day to store them into memory for yourself.

They will keep you grounded on "why" you should never give up. The days will come when you ask yourself. The opposers will ask you as well. Be prepared with the answers to get you to that finish line. That is why you deserve to be on the shelves in the aisle for (Aisle 4).

"I tell you, you can pray for anything, and if you believe that you've received it, it will be yours." Mark 11:24 NLT

Something to think about.

Success is certainly a combination of things. None of them are outward and all are within you.

Hone in on them and put them to consistent use.

STEPHANIE REMY

PLENTY OF ROOM ON THE SHELF

IX

⊙∾⊗

The Great 8

"Plant your seed in the morning and keep busy all afternoon, for you don't know if profit will come from one activity or the another – or maybe both." Ecclesiastes 11:6 NLT

You have identified your space on the shelf in the aisle. Welcome to the great eight (8). In this chapter we will explain aisle 8 in detail. There are many keys to success as there are many barriers to break down and many doors to open.

Here are what we call the **great 8 – Diligence, Determination, Devotion, Discipline, Drive, Hard Work, Ethic, Clarity**.

You need all of this in combination because many of the challenges you may face will call for them. Write them on a sticky note to serve as a constant reminder. They will get you where you're going and keep you there. Let me formally explain the great eight (8).

Diligence – (careful and persistent work or effort).
You have heard the saying when the going gets tough, well this

is what you use to push through. You will need to be diligent in your efforts because this type of persistence is essential. In the journey of life, one often encounters challenges and obstacles that test their will power. During such tough times, the phrase "when the going gets tough" takes on significant meaning. To successfully navigate through these trying moments, individuals rely on a powerful virtue called diligence. Diligence refers to the careful and persistent application of work or effort towards achieving a goal. It is the unwavering commitment to persevere in the face of difficulties, ensuring progress and ultimate success. In this book, we will explore the concept of diligence, its importance, and how it acts as a guiding force to help individuals overcome obstacles and achieve their objectives.

Defining Diligence

Diligence is a multifaceted quality that encompasses a deep commitment to putting forth best efforts consistently. It involves a meticulous approach to tasks, paying attention to detail, and maintaining focus on the ultimate objective. Diligence is not merely about working hard; it also encompasses working smart, efficiently allocating time and resources. By combining hard work and intelligence, diligence optimizes the chances of reaching desired outcomes.

The Role of Diligence in Overcoming Obstacles

1. Maintaining Resilience: When the going gets tough, it is easy to become disheartened and consider giving up. Diligence empowers individuals to stay resilient in the face of adversity. By persistently chipping away at the obstacles, one can eventually break through barriers that seemed insurmountable.

2. Learning and Growth: Diligence promotes a growth mindset. It encourages individuals to embrace challenges as

opportunities for learning and self-improvement. Through careful and persistent effort, people can develop new skills and deepen their understanding of various subjects, which, in turn, enhances their chances of success.

3. Building Confidence: Accomplishing tasks through diligent efforts boosts self-confidence. As individuals witness their progress and achievements, their belief in their capabilities strengthens. This newfound confidence becomes an invaluable asset for tackling even more significant challenges in the future.

4. Fostering Discipline: Diligence goes hand in hand with discipline. To maintain consistent effort, individuals must adhere to routines and schedules, resisting distractions that might derail their progress. This discipline translates into higher productivity and efficiency in all aspects of life.

The Relationship between Diligence and Success.

Diligence and success share a profound connection. The road to success is often riddled with setbacks, uncertainties, and obstacles. Those who demonstrate diligence are better equipped to face these challenges head-on, adapt to changing circumstances, and persevere until their goals are accomplished.

Diligence plays a pivotal role in personal growth and self-improvement. Whether it's adopting healthy habits, learning a new skill, or overcoming personal challenges, careful and persistent effort leads to positive transformation.

Diligence is a fundamental virtue that holds the power to shape destinies and create a profound impact on one's life. The commitment to applying careful and persistent work or effort is essential, particularly when facing challenges and adversities. Diligence empowers individuals to persevere in the pursuit of their goals, fostering resilience, discipline, and self-confidence along the way.

Success is not an overnight phenomenon but rather the result of consistent and determined progress towards a long-term vision. Diligence separates those who strive for excellence from those who settle for mediocrity. It enables individuals to seize opportunities, enhance problem-solving skills, and realize their aspirations in various aspects of life, be it academics, career, entrepreneurship, or personal development.

To sum up, when the going gets tough, it is diligence that provides the strength and determination to push through and keep going, ultimately leading you to the achievement of your dreams and aspirations. Embracing diligence as a guiding principle empowers individuals to overcome obstacles and reach new heights, turning the pursuit of success into a rewarding and fulfilling journey.

Determination – (firmness of purpose; resoluteness).

Standing firm on what you want to accomplish and not allowing deterrents in, is key to remaining determined. You know the goal and you are constantly getting one step closer. Stick to your purpose. This will help you stay on course. Mind over matter of fact. The message centers around the concept of determination, which is defined as "firmness of purpose." It emphasizes the importance of standing firm on what you want to accomplish and not allowing deterrents to derail your progress. Remaining determined is seen as a key factor in achieving your goals and aspirations.

When you possess determination, it means you are unwavering in your commitment to your objectives. You have a clear understanding of what you want to achieve, and you are steadfastly moving towards it. Regardless of the obstacles or challenges that come your way, you maintain focus and resilience, refusing to be discouraged or swayed from your path.

To stay determined, it's crucial to constantly remind yourself of your ultimate goal. Visualize the desired outcome, and let that vision drive you forward. Keep your purpose in mind at all times, and let it be the guiding force that propels you through difficult times.

First you need to understand that determination is a mindset, where "mind over matter" comes into play. This means that your mental attitude and fortitude are essential in overcoming any physical or external hurdles. By believing in yourself and maintaining a positive outlook, you can overcome the most challenging situations.

Pretty much, in your case determination is about standing firm on your purpose and remaining focused in the face of adversities. It includes a clear understanding of your objectives. It means staying focused on them, and not allowing anything to distract you. With the right mindset, you can overcome obstacles and stay on course to achieve your goals. So, stay determined, and let your unwavering spirit guide you to success.

Devotion – (love, loyalty, or enthusiasm for a person, activity, or cause).

This vision, this business or product is yours and yours alone. Personally, you have a loyalty to it. You have an inherent connection to it. You love it and the thought of its growth and success makes you happy. You must be devoted to your vision and your goals. If not, then any small pin like thing will burst your bubble. Keep steadfast and always understand how much this means to you, even when the world doesn't quite understand yet.

In the realm of success, there is a powerful force that sets the extraordinary apart from the ordinary – devotion. Devotion is more than just a word; it embodies love, loyalty, and an unwavering enthusiasm for a cause, an activity, or in this case, your vision, your business, or your product.

Picture this: you hold in your hands the seeds of a dream, a vision that is uniquely yours. This endeavor is not merely a concept; it runs through the very core of your being. You feel a profound connection to it, as if it were an extension of yourself. You love it dearly, nurturing it with passion and dedication, because it ignites a fire within you like nothing else.

The idea of witnessing its growth and success fills your heart with joy. It's not just a fleeting infatuation; it's a profound, enduring love that fuels your actions and choices. You know deep down that this vision is meant to flourish, and you're determined to see it bloom into reality.

But, my dear dreamer, let me share this pure wisdom with you: devotion is not a minimal passion; it is an unbreakable bond. Similar to the roots of a large tree, your devotion keeps you grounded in the face of challenges, doubts, and setbacks. When the world casts doubt on you and your dreams, and when naysayers question your vision, your devotion acts as a shield.

You must cradle this vision close to your heart, nurturing it with your utmost loyalty. It is up to only you to stay the course and execute your mission. Treat it like a precious gem, in a world of vague desires and fickle interests, devotion is the rock that stands the tides of uncertainty.

Yes, there may be obstacles, setbacks, and moments of doubt. But fear not, for your unwavering commitment will serve as a beacon, guiding you through the darkest hours. Remember, even the smallest pinprick of doubt can burst a fragile bubble. But with devotion, you create a fortress that can withstand the storms of skepticism.

So, remain determined, stand firm in your devotion. Embrace the essence of what this vision means to you. Feel the love and loyalty rushing through your veins. Your heart's connection to this purpose is what will propel you forward, even when the world fails to understand your vision.

In the grand scheme of things, those who stay true to their devoted dreams are the ones who change the world. So, keep your head high, your heart aflame, and let your devotion be the unwavering force that carries you to the pinnacle of success. Trust in your vision, and watch as it transforms from a dream to a legacy that will leave an undeniable mark on the world.

Discipline – (a code of behavior).

This key will in one way or another open all the doors. Understanding how important this function is will save you from uneasiness and feelings of unrest. It is easy to lose track and forget. But training yourself to continue on and repetitiously get back up is a high valued factor.

Discipline will be in the form of you being faced with a challenge and remembering how you used your why to overcome the last one. You will then naturally use the answers to the why "in you" to overcome this one and the next one, and any other one to come. Recall I asked you to recite the answers to your why's, doing that is discipline. That is the best way to retain the mindset to get you through things without a second thought. You will have trained your mind and body to withstand because it can.

Your mind will automatically recall the code of behavior you trained it to. Discipline is a key that will in one way or another open all the doors. Understanding how important this function is will save you from uneasiness. It is easy to lose track and forget. But training yourself to continue on and repetitiously get back up is a highly effective behavior.

It becomes like a reflex, an instinct, where you act with purpose and determination. Each challenge you face will no longer seem impossible to overcome, but rather an opportunity to apply the principles that have helped you in the past.

Life is full of uncertainties and hurdles, but with discipline, you equip yourself with a powerful tool to confront them. When others might fall or give in to despair, you will stand tall and face adversity head-on. The code of behavior you have imprinted upon yourself becomes a source of strength, guiding you towards making the right decisions, staying focused on your goals, and achieving what others might see as impossible.

Remember, discipline is not just about adhering to a set of rules or following a routine; it's a way of life. It's the mastery of self-control, the ability to stay committed even when the path ahead seems tough, and the determination to keep pushing forward seems like a hassle.

The journey of discipline will not always be smooth; there will be moments of doubt and many moments of weakness. But that's when your training will truly shine. You'll recognize those moments as opportunities for growth, for reinforcing your resolve, and for reinforcing your "why."

So, in the face of challenges, when the world seems to conspire against you, hold fast to the behavior you've cultivated through discipline. Embrace the struggles as chances to prove to yourself what you're truly capable of achieving. As you conquer each obstacle with an abundance of determination, you'll witness your inner strength blossom like never before.

Keep in mind that discipline is not an end in itself; it's a means to unlock your full potential, to lead a more purposeful and fulfilling life. With discipline by your side, you'll become the architect of your destiny, crafting a future filled with achievements, growth, and self-discovery.

So, whenever you feel like giving up, remember this message, and let it serve as a reminder: Discipline - a code of behavior. The key that opens all doors. The key that will transform your life and empower you to embrace all challenges that come your way. Embrace discipline, and you'll unleash your true potential.

Drive – (an innate, biologically determined urge to attain a goal or satisfy a need).

In order to attain that goal, you need this key. This is the gas that keeps you going. The high-quality fuel that protects your mental engine from burnout. Instead, it pushes to get you over all the hurdles without getting you off track. You know the objective and your goals are now aligned. Your drive will get you where you're going. Without it, you will just stay parked or even in a neutral position.

Stay driven because it is a motivating aspect of all your focus. Picture this: you have a destination in mind, a goal that fills you with excitement and purpose. But in order to reach that endpoint, there is a key that you simply cannot do without. It's the very essence of motivation that propels you forward, the fuel that ignites your spirit and keeps you moving steadfast towards your dreams.

This key is what separates the extraordinary from the ordinary. It's the driving force that pushes you beyond your limits, beyond the hurdles that may try to obstruct your path. When you possess this high-quality fuel, your mental engine becomes invincible, fortified against the threat of burnout and fatigue.

With this newfound power, you become an unstoppable force, fearlessly taking on challenges and surmounting them with unwavering determination. It's this very drive that keeps you firmly on course, ensuring you don't stray or veer away from your aspirations.

Embrace this driving force, for it aligns your objectives and goals in perfect harmony. It's the magnetic pull that keeps you focused, preventing distractions from steering you off track. As long as you keep your eyes locked on that end goal, nothing can deter you.

Believe in your capabilities and hold tight to the power of this motivation. With it, you'll soar to heights you never thought possible. This motivation is what will elevate you from standing still or being stuck in a neutral position. It propels you into action, daring you to exceed your own expectations.

So, stay driven and let this unwavering determination become the heartbeat of your ambitions. In moments of doubt or weariness, when you're tired and just want to give up. Those days will come, draw strength from the knowledge that this motivation is the life and blood of your success.

Embrace this truth, and you'll find that challenges are no longer fearful obstacles but stepping stones on your path to greatness. Your focus will be sharpened, and your dreams will become the very air you breathe.

Remember, it all starts with staying driven. This relentless pursuit of your goals will ignite a fire within you that burns brighter with each passing day. So, keep pushing, keep striving, and keep that drive alive. You are destined for greatness, and this motivation will be the guiding star that leads you there.

Hard Work – (a great deal of effort or endurance).

Nothing worth having comes easy. If no one ever told you that before, let me clue you in. The level of effort you put in will always show in the end. If you're in a race but instead choose to sit on the curb because you're tired, you can't win. If you keep tripping and decide it's too frustrating and give up, you can't win. If you see everyone passing you and get discouraged, you just can't win! Hard work is all the effort you put in to continue on. It's you getting tired but keep running because you push yourself closer to that one last step, every time. It's watching your fellows run past you and being inspired to keep running as well. It is having the level of frustration from constantly tripping but always getting back up and enduring every slip. When you cross that finish line you will thank yourself. The message I want to drive home is this: Nothing worth having comes easy. This is a fundamental truth in life that many may have heard before, but it cannot be emphasized enough. Whether it's success, achievement, happiness, or personal growth, genuine and lasting rewards require effort, dedication, and perseverance.

If you've never heard this message before, it's time to understand the significance. The level of effort you put in will always manifest in the end result. Just like in a race, sitting on the curb because you're tired won't lead to victory. Giving up when faced with obstacles won't get you closer to your goals either. Success demands hard work and determination.

The path to achievement is not smooth; it's filled with hurdles, setbacks, and frustrations. But hard work is precisely what keeps you moving forward. It's about pushing yourself, even when you're exhausted, taking that one last step every time. It's the resilience to get back up every time you stumble and keeping at it, moving forward despite the slips and falls. It's climbing that mountain even though you're halfway and can't seem to find the strength.

All this might seem tough, but remember, when you eventually cross that finish line, you'll understand why it was worth it. The feeling of accomplishment and the sense of pride will make all the effort, fatigue, and frustration pale in comparison.

So, embrace the challenges, endure the hardships, and maintain your determination. Embody the spirit of hard work, and when you reach your goals, you'll look back and be grateful for the journey you undertook. Every step, every fall, and every push will have been worth it. Success and fulfillment await those who put in the effort and never give up.

It will all have been worth it.

Ethic – (a set of moral principles, especially ones relating to or affirming a specified group, field, or form of conduct).

Morals keep you grounded on so many levels. Having a set of principles that you follow to get and keep you on track is important. If you are ethically sound, so many things will align. Your answers to the whys will come so easy and you will have solid ground to stand on. Your work ethic - being how hard you work at something. Your business ethic – being the principles and values you look to bring; will all help you hone in on your tribe and ultimately lead to and keep them by you. This is a valuable key to your success.

The message I want to emphasize is the significance of ethics in life, particularly in the context of personal conduct, work ethic, and business principles. Ethics refer to a set of moral principles that guide an individual or a group's behavior. They act as a moral compass, keeping you grounded and on the right path in various aspects of life.

Having a strong set of morals is crucial because they provide a framework for decision-making and behavior. When you follow ethical principles, many aspects of your life align harmoniously. You'll find it easier to answer questions about why you do what you do because your actions are guided by a clear and principled approach.

Work ethic, which pertains to how hard you work at something, is deeply influenced by your ethical foundation. When you uphold ethical values in your work, you're more likely to be diligent, responsible, and committed. This dedication not only benefits your personal growth but also earns you respect and trust from others.

This emphasis on ethics is a key factor in your overall success. It lays the foundation for sustainable growth and helps you navigate challenges with integrity and confidence. When you are ethically sound, you'll have solid ground to stand on even in the face of adversity, and your actions will be guided by a sense of purpose and fairness.

In conclusion, embracing a strong ethical framework in your personal life, work, and business is not just a virtue but a valuable key to unlocking your true potential. By following a set of moral principles and conducting yourself with integrity, you will find yourself on a path that leads to success and surrounds you with a tribe of like-minded individuals who support and believe in you.

Clarity – (the quality of being certain or definite).

First make it make sense to you. Whatever it is. Then you can make it make sense to the world. When you take time for yourself to translate your dream, and put your goals into words, you now have a clear understanding. With a clear understanding you are now able to relay and translate your message to the world. Remember whatever goal or objective you have been called towards, will need to make sense to you even if moderately. From there you will be able to explain it to the world.

All may not grasp it, but so long as you do, it will be on you to bring the vision to life. Sit quietly sometimes and listen to your breathing just to clear your mind. From there allow the thought process to take place. A clear mind is a space for things to best be defined and a place where the vision will look the most vivid. Mental clarity and clarity on the objective are all keys to the win.

You'll soon understand why you belong on the shelf. In the space that was designed for you.

"Lazy people want much but get little, but those who work hard will prosper." Proverbs 13:4 NLT

Something good is about to happen!

Check you out!
Thriving. Growing. Inspiring.
Shining like the bright star you
are. We always knew you would
make it this far!

STEPHANIE REMY

PLENTY OF ROOM ON THE SHELF

X

The Checkout Lane

"My thoughts are nothing like your thoughts," says the Lord "and my ways are far beyond anything you could imagine." Isaiah 55:8 NLT

You made it!

This is further than most. Many have tried. Many more have given up after tiredness or even failure never to try again. But you made it to checkout lane. This is where you want to make it. Where all of your successes are real and tangible and you get to take them with you wherever you go. From the vision in the mind. Through all the many challenges. With the encouragement of the cheering section. Even through the disbelief of the many opposers.

Look to your left and to your right. your fellows have made it too.

They sit beside you able to share some of the same challenges and struggles. They can relate to all the blood, sweat and tears it took to get here. They have found their tribe just as you have. In some instances, you may even have members of the same tribe. You cry tears of joy, buy you also rejoice with laughter.

All without disruption of the others on the way. All without animosity, discord, jealousy or hate, you sit side by side both winning. Both having crossed that finish line.

I tell you this, making it across the finish line, regardless the time it may have taken, is a truly rewarding feeling.

You will feel accomplished, overjoyed, proud.

As do every member of the cheering squad who always knew you had it in you. Opposers will see, and may be inspired. They may even become a member of your tribe. It's just funny how life works. But you made it to the checkout line. Found your space on the shelf in your designated aisle. You're on your way to many, many wins.

This is one of the many doors you have officially opened. Once you make it here, the work is not done. You still have to continue with all of the great eights. Your Diligence, Determination, Devotion, Discipline, Drive, Hard Work, Ethic, and Clarity will keep you in line and on track. If ever you are prompted to give up, opt out because giving up didn't get you here. Therefore, giving up is not an option. Understanding that aisles are like different stores (beauty, grocery, clothing, automotive) and the shelves like lanes you'll always understand that there will always be a place for you.

Do exactly what you want to do, whenever you want to do it. Allow yourself to feel what you feel, allow your thoughts to be free and uncloud your judgement. Everything that is meant to be will always be and you'll get everything destiny has in store for you.

Now just believe in yourself.
Your spot on the shelf is secured!

"So let's not get tired of doing what is good. At just the right time we will reap a harvest of blessing if we don't give up." Galatians 6:9 NLT

My hope for you is that this little book helps you make *BIG* strides in this world. Use it as a reminder and a resource when you need things to make sense or when you need a little pick me up. Just keep going, keep moving forward and don't look back!

STEPHANIE REMY
PLENTY OF ROOM ON THE SHELF

MAKE BIG THINGS HAPPEN!

Self-Noted Lesson

Journal

_____
_____
_____
_____
_____
_____
_____
_____
_____
_____
_____
_____
_____
_____
_____
_____
_____
_____
_____
_____
_____
_____
_____
_____
_____

_____
_____
_____
_____
_____
_____
_____
_____
_____
_____
_____
_____
_____
_____
_____
_____
_____
_____
_____
_____
_____
_____
_____
_____
_____
_____

PLENTY OF ROOM ON THE SHELF

Self-Noted Change 🩶

Journal

_____
_____
_____
_____
_____
_____
_____
_____
_____
_____
_____
_____
_____
_____
_____
_____
_____
_____
_____
_____
_____
_____
_____
_____
_____
_____

PLENTY OF ROOM ON THE SHELF

So much to be proud of...

So much to be proud of...

XI

❧

In Conclusion

Being able to identify things in your life that make you proud, will help you trust that good will come to you. I am not talking about magically appear from the open sky and fall into your lap. But rather, through the work and keeping with consistency, things that you aspire for with hard work will in fact come to fruition.

Look at the little things and how they came to be and you will find that they are not so small after all. In the appreciation of small things, greater things come to be as well. Your growth is inevitable, so keep pushing and achieve what is yours to achieve. Get comfortable being uncomfortable. It is in your stuck state, that you find a way to get unstuck. I hope you take from this book all that it has to offer. Use the tools and put them to work for you. Refer to the resources and tap into what you have access to. I always tell clients, there is no way you were just put here on this earth to just be. You have a purpose and a role to play, so play it out!

I do not accept defeat, and I will not allow you to succumb to your own doubt, failure, frustrations or even to the onlookers who are naysayers. If you fail, try again. If you fall, get back up! If you get lost, keep looking for the way out. If you tire, rest, but no matter what just do not stop moving. A winner never quits, and a quitter never wins – what a true statement. You can't win a race you don't run and you most definitely have zero chance winning a race you don't start. Standing by on the sidelines doesn't offer a trophy at the end. This is what I want you to recognize and steer away from.

Nothing worth having will be hand delivered to your door without you playing a part. Even a pizza has to be ordered before being delivered to your door. Items have to be ordered before being shipped and delivered to your door. Well just as that, the work needs to be put in so that success can come ringing your door bell, and banging at your door.

At the start of the day, if it means something to you, you will do whatever it takes. You will push, pull, fall, get up, fail, fail again, try again, fail some more all in order to succeed. The victory at the end always looks simple to those who were not on the journey. Even with visible battle scars, dripping sweat and evident tears all they can see is the victory. You Won! This is why your only option is success. The path you took and whatever happened along the way does not hold much weight, your results are how you're certified. It is what the world gets to see.

So, at the end of the day, prior to closing your eyes, decide what you are willing to do when you wake up, in order to succeed. Planning is an essential way to get closer to success. I'll save planning techniques for another book, as it stands you have already got some work to do.

Let's identify Goals and Objectives.

Let me leave you with this. Going back to what was is not an option, so in reality looking forward and creating a different ending is!

"For God has not given us a spirit of fear and timidity, but of power, love, and self-discipline." 2 Timothy 1:7 NLT

Let's get started!

Objectives and Goals ♥

_____

_____

_____

_____

_____

_____

_____

_____

_____

_____

_____

_____

_____

_____

_____

_____

_____

_____

_____

_____

_____

_____

_____

PLENTY OF ROOM ON THE SHELF

Objectives and Goals

Objectives and Goals

♥

_____

_____

_____

_____

_____

_____

_____

_____

_____

_____

_____

_____

_____

_____

_____

_____

_____

_____

_____

_____

_____

_____

Objectives and Goals

♥

_____

_____

_____

_____

_____

_____

_____

_____

_____

_____

_____

_____

_____

_____

_____

_____

_____

_____

_____

_____

_____

_____

_____

_____

_____

My reasons WHY

_____

_____

_____

_____

_____

_____

_____

_____

_____

_____

_____

_____

_____

_____

_____

_____

_____

_____

_____

_____

_____

My reasons WHY

Members of my Cheering Squad

_____

_____

_____

_____

_____

_____

_____

_____

_____

_____

_____

_____

_____

_____

_____

_____

_____

_____

_____

_____

_____

_____

_____

PLENTY OF ROOM ON THE SHELF

Members of my Cheering Squad

So much to be proud of...

♥

_____

_____

_____

_____

_____

_____

_____

_____

_____

_____

_____

_____

_____

_____

_____

_____

_____

_____

_____

_____

_____

_____

So much to be proud of...

♡

_____

_____

_____

_____

_____

_____

_____

_____

_____

_____

_____

_____

_____

_____

_____

_____

_____

_____

_____

_____

_____

_____

_____

Pray - Meditate - Manifest

Let me share my secret recipe with you.

Reading this book you have probably come to realize I use biblical verses to support many of my claims.

I believe in the power of prayer, meditation, and affirming words of positivity.

Thoughts can be powerful as can your words. The power in the tongue and things that you speak have a way of coming to be. Manifesting they call it.

Being positive, from your state of mind to your state of being are all relative.

Life can give you everything you ask of it. Be specific and clear, remain consistent and it does deliver.

I pray often and am intentional about my requests. I speak what I seek, until I see what I say. Even noting when I do not speak my needs they do not come to pass. In my prayer I make my requests and desires known. Thoughts are equally strong. The more you think about something, you will eventually vocalize the thought. Thus allowing it to come to be a reality, one often unexpected and unwelcome by you.

We may wonder why and how something that happens to us comes to pass, and it may lead back to a multitude of times of reciting the same negative statements once thought. When facing different circumstances many people believe the "woe is me" and repeat it time after time. People strum on their negativity, it lingers in their thoughts, they wallow in sorrow and recite negative thoughts. This in turn manifests into their truth.

Pray about things. Ask for discernment to ensure things make sense. Seek spiritual guidance that may speak to you as the sound and feeling of that inner voice. Trust it.

Your gut doesn't lie, it makes you uneasy in order to steer you away from certain things.

The spirit of the Lord has a way of offering signs and putting things on your path to clear the way. Trust that what you pray for will be revealed to you. He is intentional and makes no mistakes.

Affirm your understanding that all this is true.

Affirm that all that is revealed to you is REAL.

Affirm that you are deserving of the goodness your heart desires.

Affirmations are your consistent reminders. In this book we use "I understand" instead of "I am" because an understanding is a firm affirmation of truth. An accepted version of the true intentions you see for your life.

Pray.
Don't worry about anything; instead, pray about everything. Tell God what you need, and thank him for all he has done **Philippians 4:6 NLT**

Meditate.
May the words of my mouth and the meditation of my heart be pleasing to you, O LORD, my rock and my redeemer. **Psalms 19:14 NLT**

Manifest.
Faith shows the reality of what we hope for; it is the evidence of things we cannot see.
Hebrews 11:1 NLT

Affirmations

:

I understand that my life is destined with a story

I understand that everything for me is already mine

I understand that the work to be done will be done by me

I understand that jealousy and envy are not my way of life

I understand that there is a reservation of my spot on the shelf of success

I understand that I am already an inspiration

I understand that my greatest goals will come to pass

I understand that my goals and dreams are worth my pursuit

I understand that my reasons why will be my source of truth

I understand that all my hard work will pay off

PLENTY OF ROOM ON THE SHELF

Soon you'll realize, sometimes a little reminder is all you needed.

(Repeat as often as necessary)

Self-Care Checklist Guide

The following section is to help encourage you to identify ways to meet your self care needs. It is broken down into 21 days. Studies have shown that this is the amount of time it takes to develop a new habit. If not putting your needs at the top of your priorities has been an issue, let's correct that.

Please make the time in your busy schedule to cultivate this habit and improve yourself.

The first few pages are prefilled and merely call for checking off the item. If you have done one of the listed actions for yourself, just check it off. It is OK if you are unable to complete every task the objective here is to ensure you at least consider yourself throughout the day. Use this as a roadmap. Some items on the checklist may seem obvious and common knowledge for most, but don't hang on to that. Keep in mind when facing countless challenges and having a clouded mind so many of the simple things can easily be forgotten.

Let's give each other some grace. Life happens in it's very own way and some days we all fall short. Consider the checklist as a gentle reminder. Simple things that just aren't as simple when the priorities do not align. We understand that so use this checklist to help you hone in on little things. All the little things within your reach.

Sections:

1. **Goal:** Write down a short goal for the day. (i.e. be happy, be inspired, feel good, be thankful)
2. **Date**: Make note of the date for tracking.
3. **Checklist:** Write down things you can do for yourself to meet the goal of the day.

Be generous with yourself.
Be considerate of yourself.
Be loving to yourself.

Self-Care
CHECKLIST

Goal : _Feel content_

Date : _____

Do something for yourself today!

- ○ Say a prayer
- ○ Take a shower
- ○ Brush your teeth
- ○ Fix your hair
- ○ Put on a nice outfit
- ○ Have breakfast
- ○ Go for a walk
- ○ Do Yoga
- ○ Read a book
- ○ Go workout
- ○ Spend time with loved ones
- ○ Treat yourself to something
- ○ Watch a funny movie
- ○ Meditate = Silence your mind

elf-Care
CHECKLIST

Goal : Gratefulness

Date :

Do something for yourself today!

- ○ Say a prayer
- ○ Take a shower
- ○ Brush your teeth
- ○ Fix your hair
- ○ Put on a nice outfit
- ○ Have breakfast
- ○ Go for a walk
- ○ Journal
- ○ Pamper yourself
- ○ Rest
- ○ Try a new recipe
- ○ Do a good deed
- ○ Recite Affirmations
- ○ Meditate = Silence your mind

Self-Care
CHECKLIST

Goal : *Feel ease*

Date :

Do something for yourself today!

- ○ Say a prayer
- ○ Take a shower
- ○ Brush your teeth
- ○ Fix your hair
- ○ Put on a nice outfit
- ○ Have breakfast
- ○ Do Yoga
- ○ Go for a walk
- ○ Disconnect from digital
- ○ Read a book
- ○ Go to the mall
- ○ Be inspired by nature
- ○ Laugh in the mirror
- ○ Go to bed early

elf-Care
CHECKLIST

Goal : *Feel inspired*

Date :

Do something for yourself today!

- ○ Say a prayer
- ○ Take a bath - soak
- ○ Brush your teeth
- ○ Fix your hair
- ○ Put on a nice outfit
- ○ Eat some fruit
- ○ Smile for 30 seconds
- ○ Go for a walk
- ○ Listen to music
- ○ Recite Affirmations
- ○ Do 10 Jumping Jacks
- ○ Try a new food item
- ○ Tell yourself a funny joke
- ○ Say a prayer... again

Self-Care
CHECKLIST

Goal : _Be happy_

Date : _____

Do something for yourself today?

- ○ Say a prayer
- ○ Recite Affirmations
- ○ Take a shower
- ○ Brush your teeth
- ○ Fix your hair
- ○ Put on a nice outfit
- ○ Make a smoothie
- ○ Read a book
- ○ Go to the gym
- ○ Make a new friend
- ○ Watch a funny movie
- ○ Do 25 Jumping Jacks
- ○ Bake something
- ○ Sit quietly.

elf-Care
CHECKLIST

Goal :

Date :

Do something for yourself today!

- ○ Say a prayer
- ○
- ○
- ○
- ○
- ○
- ○
- ○ Go for a walk
- ○
- ○
- ○
- ○
- ○
- ○

Self-Care
CHECKLIST

Goal :
Date :

Do something for yourself today?

○ Say a prayer

○

○

○

○

○

○

○

○

○

○

○

○

elf-Care
CHECKLIST

Goal. :

Date :

Do something for yourself today!

- ◯ Say a prayer
- ◯
- ◯
- ◯
- ◯ Put on a nice outfit
- ◯
- ◯
- ◯
- ◯
- ◯
- ◯
- ◯
- ◯

Self-Care
CHECKLIST

Goal : _____

Date : _____

Do something for yourself today!

- ○ Say a prayer
- ○ _____
- ○ _____
- ○ _____
- ○ _____
- ○ _____
- ○ _____
- ○ _____
- ○ _____
- ○ _____
- ○ _____
- ○ _____
- ○ _____
- ○ _____

elf-Care
CHECKLIST

Goal :

Date :

Do something for yourself today!

- ◯ Say a prayer
- ◯
- ◯
- ◯
- ◯
- ◯
- ◯ Meditate = Silence your mind
- ◯
- ◯
- ◯
- ◯
- ◯
- ◯
- ◯

Self-Care
CHECKLIST

Goal :　_____

Date :　_____

Do something for yourself today!

- ○　Say a prayer
- ○
- ○
- ○
- ○
- ○
- ○
- ○
- ○
- ○
- ○
- ○
- ○

Self-Care
CHECKLIST

Goal :
Date :

Do something for yourself today!

○   Say a prayer

○

○

○

○

○

○

○

○   Recite Affirmations

○

○

○

○

Self-Care
CHECKLIST

Goal :

Date :

Do something for yourself today!

- ○ Say a prayer
- ○
- ○
- ○
- ○
- ○
- ○
- ○
- ○
- ○
- ○
- ○
- ○

elf-Care
CHECKLIST

Goal :

Date :

Do something for yourself today!

- ○   Say a prayer
- ○
- ○
- ○
- ○
- ○
- ○
- ○
- ○
- ○
- ○   Say a prayer... again
- ○
- ○

Self-Care
CHECKLIST

Goal :

Date :

Do something for yourself today!

- ○ Say a prayer
- ○
- ○
- ○
- ○
- ○
- ○
- ○
- ○
- ○
- ○
- ○
- ○
- ○

elf-Care
CHECKLIST

Goal :

Date :

Do something for yourself today?

- ◯   Say a prayer
- ◯
- ◯
- ◯
- ◯
- ◯
- ◯
- ◯
- ◯
- ◯
- ◯   Do 25 Jumping Jacks
- ◯
- ◯

Self-Care
CHECKLIST

Goal :

Date :

Do something for yourself today!

- ○ Say a prayer
- ○
- ○
- ○
- ○
- ○
- ○
- ○
- ○
- ○
- ○
- ○
- ○
- ○

elf-Care
CHECKLIST

Goal :

Date :

Do something for yourself today!

- ○ Say a prayer
- ○
- ○
- ○
- ○
- ○
- ○
- ○
- ○
- ○
- ○ Treat yourself to something
- ○
- ○

Self-Care
CHECKLIST

Goal :
Date :

Do something for yourself today!

- ○ Say a prayer
- ○
- ○
- ○
- ○
- ○
- ○
- ○
- ○
- ○
- ○
- ○
- ○
- ○

elf-Care
CHECKLIST

Goal :

Date :

Do something for yourself today!

- ○ Say a prayer
- ○
- ○
- ○
- ○
- ○
- ○
- ○
- ○
- ○
- ○
- ○
- ○
- ○

Self-Care
CHECKLIST

Goal :

Date :

Do something for yourself today!

- ⭕ Say a prayer
- ⭕
- ⭕
- ⭕
- ⭕
- ⭕
- ⭕ Disconnect from digital
- ⭕
- ⭕
- ⭕
- ⭕
- ⭕
- ⭕
- ⭕

How do you feel today?

If these 21 days of self care have changed you for the better. It was a success.
If you missed the mark and feel no changes - do yourSELF a favor and try again.
That is totally fine to not hit the mark on your first try.
Check off anything you didn't do and try some of the things that worked again.

Once you have completed all 21 days AWESOME WORK!!!

Implement these changes and routine maintenance to your daily life to help support
a healthy mind, body and spirit.

Tip: Go back through and use a different color pen to check off new things you do for yourself.

A Summary of Sorts

It is important to keep yourself motivated!

Motivation is like fuel it drives your journey closer and closer to success. Throughout this book, we've explored various strategies to maintain and boost your motivation. Remember, motivation is not a constant state; it fluctuates. Here are key takeaways to help you stay motivated:

1. **Set Clear Goals**: Define what success means to you. Clear, specific goals provide direction and purpose. Refer to the "Objectives and Goals" section in this book for.

2. **Visualize Success**: Regularly imagine achieving your goals. Visualization strengthens your resolve and keeps you focused. Recite your affirmations!

3. **Celebrate Small Wins**: Acknowledge and celebrate your progress, no matter how small. These victories build momentum and confidence. This is your REMINDER to recognize the small things.

4. **Stay Positive**: Surround yourself with positivity. Replace negative thoughts with affirmations and optimistic perspectives. Everything in your environment is a contributor of both positive and negative.

5. **Continuous Learning**: Embrace lifelong learning. Knowledge and skills are critical to overcoming challenges that keep one from staying motivated.

Be supportive to be supported!

No journey to success is a solo endeavor. The people who believe in you play a crucial role in your achievements. Again, this is your quick reminder. Here's how to leverage their support:

1. **Build a Strong Network**: Surround yourself with supportive and inspiring individuals. Their belief in you can fuel your own self-belief.

2. **Seek Mentors**: Find mentors who have walked the path you aspire to tread. Their guidance and advice are invaluable.
3. **Communicate Openly**: Share your goals and challenges with your support network. Honest communication fosters understanding and encouragement.
4. **Give Back**: Support others in their journeys. Helping others can reinforce your own motivation and create a reciprocal cycle of encouragement.

Challenges and Obstacles can be overcome!

Challenges are inevitable on the road to success. How you respond to them defines your journey. Here are strategies to overcome obstacles:

1. **Stay Resilient**: Develop resilience by viewing challenges as opportunities to grow. Resilience helps you bounce back from setbacks.
2. **Problem-Solving Skills**: Enhance your ability to solve problems creatively and effectively. Approach challenges with a solution-oriented mindset.
3. **Adaptability**: Be flexible and open to change. Adaptability allows you to navigate unexpected obstacles and remain on course.
4. **Persistence**: Keep pushing forward even when the going gets tough. Persistence is a key trait of successful individuals.
5. **Seek Help When Needed**: Don't hesitate to ask for assistance. Leveraging others' expertise can provide new perspectives and solutions.

Stick it out - Stay Committed to Your Goals!

Commitment is the cornerstone of success. Here's how to maintain your dedication to your goals:

1. **Create a Plan**: Develop a detailed action plan outlining steps to achieve your goals. A clear plan keeps you organized and focused.
2. **Set Milestones**: Break your goals into manageable milestones. Milestones provide checkpoints to assess your progress and stay on track.
3. **Track Your Progress**: Regularly monitor your progress. Keeping track helps you stay accountable and make necessary adjustments.
4. **Stay Disciplined**: Cultivate discipline in your daily habits. Consistent effort and discipline are essential to long-term success.
5. **Reevaluate and Adjust**: Periodically reassess your goals and strategies. Flexibility to adjust ensures you stay aligned with your ultimate objectives.

Success is a journey, not a destination. It requires continuous effort, resilience, and a strong support system. Remember, you have the power to shape your path and achieve each one of your dreams. Just keep the following in mind:

- **Believe in Yourself**: Self-belief is the foundation of success. Trust in your abilities and your vision.
- **Embrace Failure**: Failure is not the opposite of success; it's part of the journey. Learn from your failures and use them as stepping stones.
- **Stay Inspired**: Draw inspiration from those who have achieved what you aspire to. Let their stories fuel your drive.
- **Keep Moving Forward**: No matter the obstacles, keep pushing forward. Each step brings you closer to your goals.

You are capable of achieving greatness.
Your journey to success is uniquely yours – embrace it with determination and passion.

Personally, I am already SO Proud of You!

NO TWO PATHS ARE ALIKE

Inspirational Quotes

You certainly don't have to take my words alone as your inspiration or source of truth. Here are a few additional words and quotes you can use to inspire you. Successful people throughout history had a formula, use the insight they shared to ignite the fire within you. Check this for inspiration and a reminder from time to time. There are so many ways to achieve success. It is totally fine to gather inspiration from combined ingredients to produce your own recipe.

"IF YOU CAN'T FLY THEN RUN, IF YOU CAN'T RUN THEN WALK, IF YOU CAN'T WALK THEN CRAWL, BUT WHATEVER YOU DO YOU HAVE TO KEEP MOVING FORWARD."

— Martin Luther King Jr.

"Your time is limited, so don't waste it living someone else's life."

- Steve Jobs

"Live as if you were to die tomorrow. Learn as if you were to live forever."
Mahatma Gandhi

"You will never change your life until you change something you do daily.
The secret of your success is found in your daily routine."
- John C. Maxwell

"You cannot swim for new horizons until you have the courage to lose sight of the shore."
William Faulkner

"Define success on your own terms, achieve it by your own rules, and
build a life you're proud to live."
Anne Sweeney

"Start where you are. Use what you have. Do what you can."
Arthur Ashe

"Yesterday I was clever, so I wanted to change the world.
Today I am wise, so I am changing myself." Rumi

"Abandon anything about your life and habits that might be holding you back.
Learn to create your own opportunities."
Sophia Amoruso

"Someday is not a day of the week."
Janet Dailey

"If your actions inspire others to dream more, learn more, do more
and become more, you are a leader."
John Quincy Adams

"I am not a product of my circumstances. I am a product of my decisions."
Stephen Covey

"People often say that motivation doesn't last. Well, neither does bathing
– that's why we recommend it daily."
Zig Ziglar

"The question isn't who's going to let me; it's who is going to stop me?"
Ayn Rand

"Ordinary people think merely of spending time, great people think of using it."
Arthur Schopenhauer

"I think frugality drives innovation, just like other constraints do. One of the only ways to get out of a tight box is to invent your way out."
Jeff Bezos

"We must believe that we are gifted for something and that this thing must be attained."
Marie Curie

"The future belongs to those who learn more skills and combine them in creative ways."
Robert Greene

"If you dwell on the past or future, you will miss the moment."
Rumi

"Would I rather be feared or loved? Easy. Both.
I want people to be afraid of how much they love me."
Michael Scott

"At the end of the day, you are solely responsible for your success and your failure. And the sooner you realize that, you accept that, and integrate that into your work ethic, you will start being successful. As long as you blame others for the reason you aren't where you want to be,
you will always be a failure."
Erin Cummings

"Luck is preparation meeting opportunity."
Oprah Winfrey

"Tough times never last, but tough people do."
Robert Schuller

"We are what we repeatedly do. Excellence, therefore, is not an act. But a habit."
Aristotle

"Our greatest glory is not in never falling, but in rising every time we fall."
- Confucius

"Everything you can imagine is real."
Pablo Picasso

"PRAYER IS NOT ASKING. IT IS A LONGING OF THE SOUL. IT IS DAILY ADMISSION OF ONE'S WEAKNESS. IT IS BETTER IN PRAYER TO HAVE A HEART WITHOUT WORDS THAN WORDS WITHOUT A HEART."

— Mahatma Gandhi

Born and Raised in Boston MA.

Mother to two young humans and the youngest of eleven siblings. Who would ever think the youngest would grow to be wise enough to help others see from a clear eye view? Well, you learn best from your environment, and when you take from every situation the lesson you make good with the outcomes.

A serial entrepreneur with several successful businesses including a consulting firm that develops business solutions, including coaching business owners and executives. I always understood that success was always one step away from the hard work required. It wasn't easy getting there but everything I share in this book helped me arrive. Although I am still on my journey with many more roads to go. That's reasonable as I now have a better understanding on how life works.

I have always been an advocate for people, an ear to my closest friends, a voice of reason when challenges were presented that made no sense. I found solutions to situations that often appeared as if no resolution was possible. It is rewarding for me merely seeing others overcome challenges through to their inherent potential.

It is far too easy to get lost in this big world, so my way of giving back is by helping people see in them, what may seem foggy in the mirror. Unclear through the tears and confusing after being discouraged by others, or even their own fear.

This book is to help anyone I can't reach in person get the inspiration they need to continue on. My greatest hope is that I can also help you on your life journey, even if just a little bit.